DEFENSIVE END CHANDLER JONES,
LINEBACKER DONT'A HIGHTOWER

CREATIVE EDUCATION

AARON FRISCH

NEW ENGLAND PATRIOTS

SUPER BOWL CHAMPIONS

Published by Creative Education
P.O. Box 227, Mankato, Minnesota 56002
Creative Education is an imprint of The Creative Company
www.thecreativecompany.us

Design and production by Blue Design
Art direction by Rita Marshall
Printed in the United States of America

Photographs by Getty Images (Barry Chin/The Boston
Globe, Scott Cunningham, Jim Davis/The Boston Globe,
David Drapkin, Steve Dunwell, Otto Greule Jr., Walter
Iooss Jr./Sports Illustrated, Jim McIsaac, Donald Miralle,
Ronald C. Modra/Sports Imagery, NFL Photos, Darryl
Norenberg/NFL, Joe Robbins, Jim Rogash, Damian
Strohmeyer/Sports Illustrated, Al Tielemans/Sports
Illustrated, Jared Wickerham)

Library of Congress Cataloging-in-Publication Data
Frisch, Aaron.
New England Patriots / Aaron Frisch.
p. cm. — (Super bowl champions)
Includes index.
Summary: An elementary look at the New England
Patriots professional football team, including its
formation in 1960, most memorable players, Super Bowl
championships, and stars of today.
ISBN 978-1-60818-380-7
1. New England Patriots (Football team)—History—
Juvenile literature. I. Title.

GV956.N36F75 2014
796.332'640974461—dc23
                                                2013010645

9 8 7 6 5 4 3 2

TEDY BRUSCHI / 1996-2008

Tedy was a smart linebacker. He led the defense and helped New England win three championships.

TABLE OF CONTENTS

A PATRIOTIC TEAM. 8

WELCOME TO NEW ENGLAND 11

THE TEAM OF THE 2000s 12

THE PATRIOTS' STORY 15

FACTS FILE 22

GLOSSARY 24

INDEX 24

SOUND IT OUT

BRUSCHI: *BROO-skee*

STANLEY MORGAN / 1977–89

Stanley was a speedy receiver in the 1980s. He set a team record for touchdown catches.

A PATRIOTIC TEAM

America fought a war to be free in the 1700s.
Americans who fought against England were called
Patriots. Today, people in New England cheer for
football Patriots!

FAMOUS PATRIOTS

BEN COATES / 1991-99

Ben was a tight end who scored 50 touchdowns for the Patriots. He went to the **Pro Bowl** five times.

WELCOME TO NEW ENGLAND

New England is an area in northeastern America. Many people moved from England there hundreds of years ago. Boston, Massachusetts, is the area's biggest city.

JOHN HANNAH

1973–85

John was a powerful guard. Some people think he was the best NFL offensive lineman ever.

THE TEAM OF THE 2000s

The New England Patriots became the best National Football League (NFL) team in the 2000s. They won three Super Bowls. People called them "The Team of the 2000s"!

PATRIOTS DEFENSE

STEVE GROGAN

THE PATRIOTS' STORY

The Patriots started out in 1960. They played in the
American Football League (AFL) then. The Patriots
almost won the AFL championship in 1963. In 1970,
they joined the NFL.

Tough quarterback Steve Grogan led New England
to the **playoffs** three times. The Patriots went to the
Super Bowl after the 1985 season, but they lost.

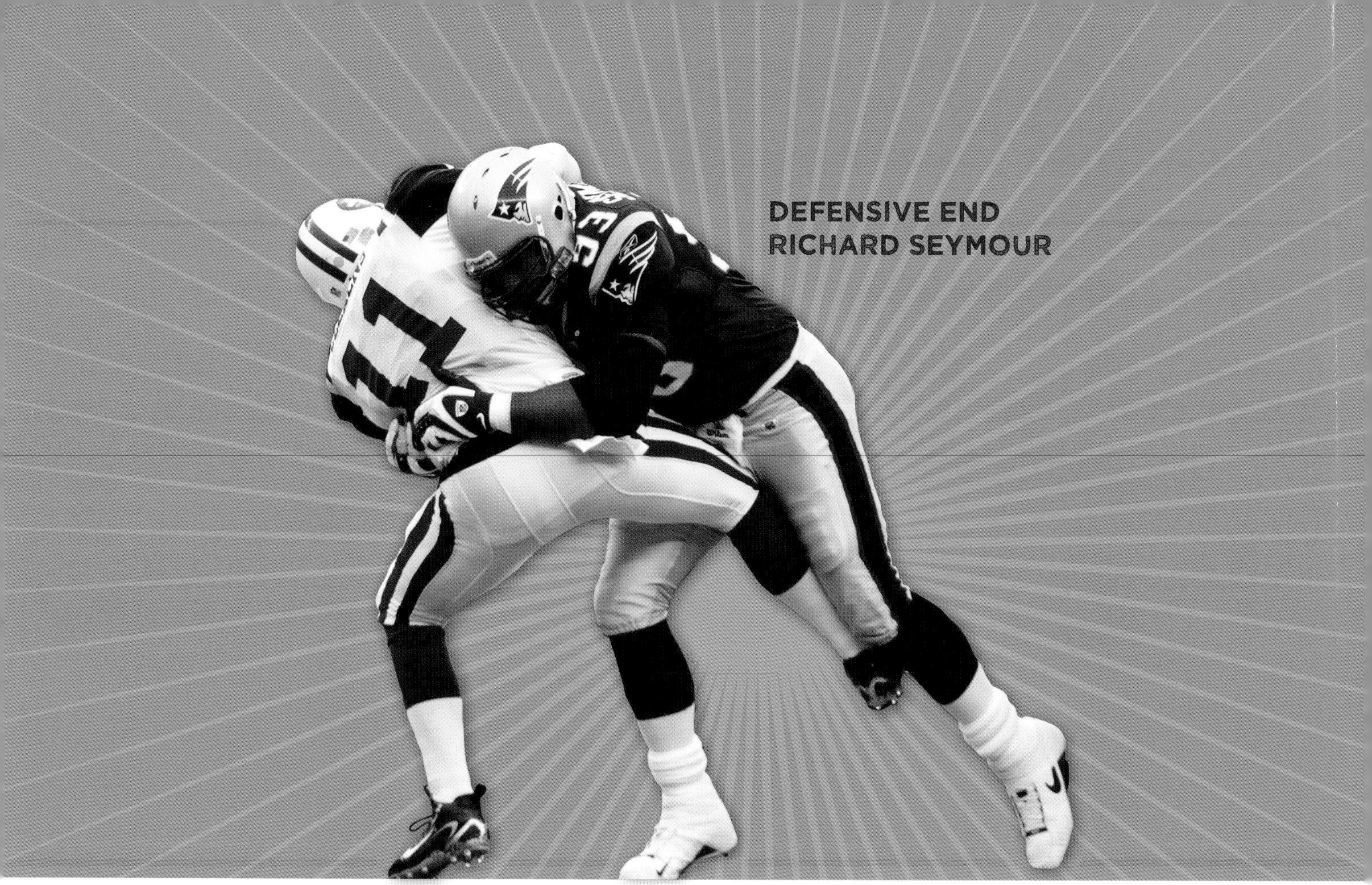

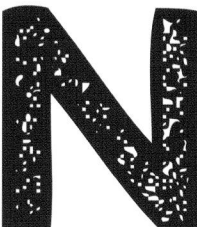

DEFENSIVE END
RICHARD SEYMOUR

New England won a lot of games in the 1990s. But the Patriots did not become champions until they added coach Bill Belichick and quarterback Tom Brady.

TOM BRADY

VINATIERI: *vin-uh-tee-AIR-ee*

VINCE WILFORK

18

ADAM VINATIERI

1996–2005

Adam was a kicker who made many field goals that helped the Patriots win Super Bowls.

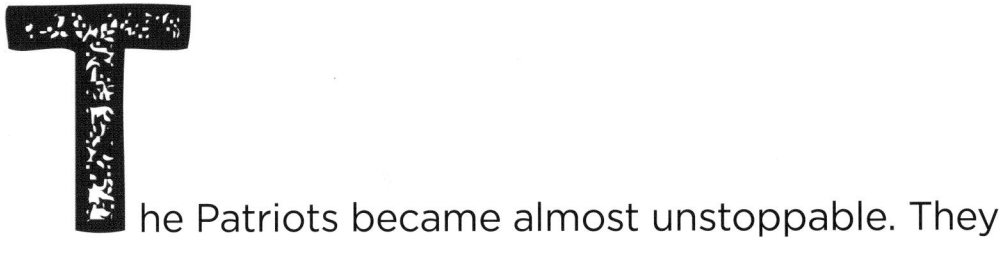

he Patriots became almost unstoppable. They won Super Bowls after the 2001, 2003, and 2004 seasons! In 2007, they won 18 games and lost only 1. New England had a lot of tough defensive players. Huge defensive tackle Vince Wilfork was a great **run stopper** for the Patriots.

**WIDE RECEIVER
WES WELKER**

In 2013, big tight end Rob Gronkowski caught a
lot of touchdown passes for New England. Rob and
his teammates fought hard to try to win another
Super Bowl!

"I watched them go to the Super Bowl as I was growing up and now I'm part of it? It is an unreal moment and you can't take it for granted."
—ROB GRONKOWSKI

GLOSSARY

playoffs — games that the best teams play after a season to see who the champion will be

Pro Bowl — a special game after the season that only the best NFL players get to play

record — something that is the most or best ever

run stopper — a defensive player who is good at stopping running backs

INDEX

AFL 15

Belichick, Bill 16

Brady, Tom 16

Bruschi, Tedy 6

Cappelletti, Gino 15

Coates, Ben 9

Grogan, Steve 15

Gronkowski, Rob 20, 21

Hannah, John 12

Morgan, Stanley 8

playoffs 15

Pro Bowl 9

Super Bowl 12, 15, 19, 22

team name 8

"Team of the 2000s" 12

team records 8

Vinatieri, Adam 19

Wilfork, Vince 19